AF483642

Danny the Diabetic Dinosaur

Danny the Diabetic Dinosaur

Published by Welch's Innovative Learning

Contact Emily Welch
W.innovativelearning@gmail.com

ISBN 979-8-218-98445-8

To Mom and Dad, for inspiring

innovation in me from day one.

- E.W.

Danny Dino was a happy little brontosaurus living in Dinoland.
He liked to run, jump, and play dinosaur games with all his friends.

One day, Danny noticed his pants were getting really big!

Not only were his pants too big, but he felt itchy in his breeches at times.

He ate and he ate, but he could not gain weight.

He told his mom, and she asked, "What other things have you been feeling, little Danny?" "Oh, Mommy, I have been so thirsty and tired. I can't sleep at night because I have to go potty all the time. I have been really hungry, and it always looks foggy outside." "Oh my, Danny, I will call Dr. Rex!"

When Danny went to Dr. Rex, he got to do all sorts of cool things. He weighed on the big scale. Dr. Rex said Danny had lost several dino pounds.

The doctor used his special listening tool to hear the *"lub dub"* of Danny's heart. He also used a tool to give Danny's arm a great big hug!

Dr. Rex finished his visit with a little prickly to test Danny's dino juices. Little Danny was so brave. He said, "It didn't even hurt."

Dr. Rex let Danny pick his very own sticker for his bravery, and he wore it proudly. Then, Dr. Rex told Danny and his mom he had type 1 diabetes, but it was not his fault.

Dr. Rex explained that Danny had a lot of glucose in his dino juices. His mom asked, "What is glucose?" Dr. Rex said, "Glucose is just a fancy word for sugar, and your body needs sugar just like a car needs gas for fuel and energy."

Danny's mom asked, "If Danny has so much sugar, why is he losing so many dino pounds and feeling so tired?"

Dr. Rex told his mom, "Danny has plenty of sugar, but his insulin delivery trucks are broke down and cannot get his sugar where it needs to go to give him energy."

Mommy Dino asked, "Why are Danny's insulin delivery trucks broke down?"
Closed
PANCREAS
Dr. Rex said, "Inside Danny's tummy is a little factory called the pancreas that is in charge of making insulin delivery trucks. Danny's pancreas is closed, and he doesn't have enough insulin trucks working to deliver all his sugar."

Dr. Rex told Danny and his mom it would all be okay, and Danny would soon play again. He said Danny would need to check his dino juices with a little finger prickly and his special dinomatic sugar reader before meals, exercise, and bedtime.

Dr. Rex told Danny he would need to compare his dinomatic sugar score with an insulin chart he would give him. Danny could use the chart to see if he needed to eat a healthy snack or take insulin through a little prickly that his parents, school nurse, or dino-sitter would help him with.

Dr. Rex sent Danny on a great journey with a map to learn all about how to live a healthy life with type 1 diabetes. Danny was so excited to go on a learning adventure and meet new friends.

On his first stop, Danny met Tony the triceratops working in his vegetable garden. "Hey, Danny," Tony said, "these vegetables are full of good sugar for energy to help you run and play. Please take some of my prize-winning vegetables for your journey." Proudly carrying his vegetables, Danny set out for his next stop.

Along his path, he met Roxy Rex who had just opened a fresh meat market. Roxy was excited to show him her selection of fish, chicken, and beef. She told him about the importance of protein in his diet. She said, "Protein helps build strong muscles and keep healthy sugar scores." She gave him some chicken and fish for his bag.

At his next stop, he went to Dexter's dairy farm. Dexter was thrilled to tell Danny all about his milk and cheese. Danny learned dairy products help build strong bones. He selected some of Dexter's finest milk and cheese to take home.
Dexter's Dairy
SALE
MILK
Danny

Danny then went to Fred's fruit stand. Fred said, "Fruits are a great source of healthy sugar. They taste sweet and are full of great energy. You should eat fruits daily, but they are high in sugar, so watch your sugar score closely. Also, fruit juice can be a great way to increase your sugar score if you ever feel shaky or weak."

When Danny looked at his map, he only had four stops left. He was on the road to Brenda's Bakery. He could smell the freshly baked bread in the air. Brenda was so happy to see Danny when he arrived. She gave him a slice of whole grain bread and some nuts for a snack.

Brenda taught Danny all about carbohydrates which come from bread, rice, oats, and even fruits and vegetables. She said, "They are all forms of sugar that give you energy for the day." Danny would need to eat these foods daily for energy.

Danny was very excited about his next stop. He was going to Claire's Candy Shop! "Welcome, Danny," Claire said. "Dr. Rex said you would be coming." Danny was so excited to try all the candy, but Claire taught him that he should only eat sweets in small amounts. However, he should keep a few pieces of candy or glucose tablets with him for if he ever felt low or funny.

Dr. Rex said Danny would know if he needed to eat sugar if his dinomatic sugar score was low and he had shaky legs, was sweaty, or felt really tired. He should tell his parents or a trusted adult if he ever felt funny or low. Claire gave him a little bag of candy to take home.

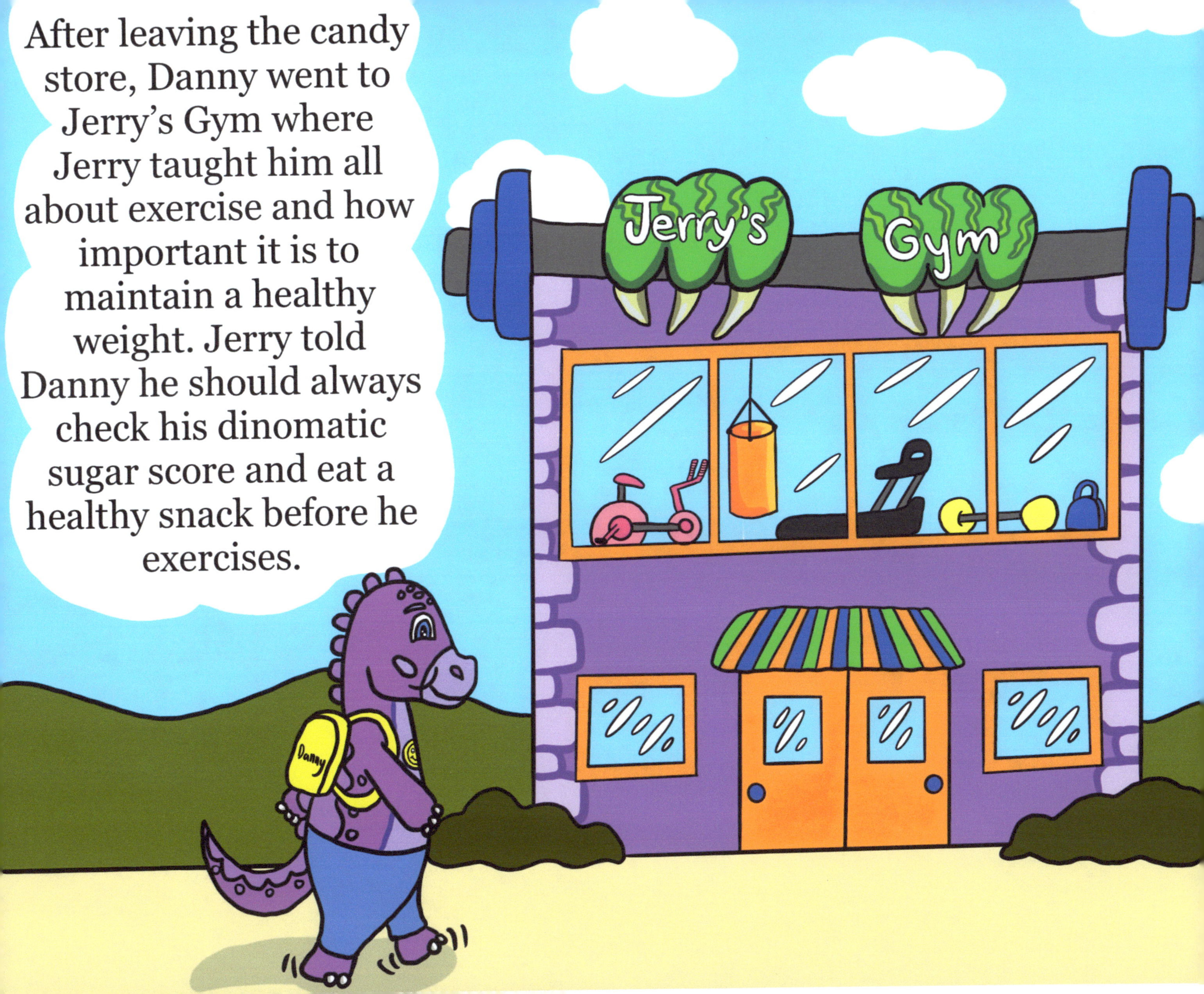

After leaving the candy store, Danny went to Jerry's Gym where Jerry taught him all about exercise and how important it is to maintain a healthy weight. Jerry told Danny he should always check his dinomatic sugar score and eat a healthy snack before he exercises.
Jerry's Gym
Danny

Jerry said, "If you get weak while exercising, Dr. Rex said you should do another finger prickly to check your dino juices. Remember to always tell your parents, teacher, nurse, or dino-sitter how you are feeling." Jerry gave Danny a jump rope so he could exercise with his friends.
Danny
Water
Protein

Danny's final stop was at Buddy's Book Store. "Hello, Danny, I have been waiting for you. I have a special gift just for you and your mom. I want you to take this journal home so you can tell your mom everything you eat and she can write it down. This will help you keep track of your food and how they affect your dino juice sugar levels. Dr. Rex wanted me to remind you to always tell your parents what you eat so they can write it down."

"Thank you, Buddy and everyone! I can't wait to go home and show my mom everything you all have given me and tell her everything I have learned."
Danny
Buddy's Books

"Look Mom, I got all this stuff on my great adventure. I have learned all about the foods I can eat to stay healthy and how to safely exercise. Buddy gave me a journal to write down what I eat." "Oh, Danny, I am so proud of you! Dr. Rex will be so excited at your next visit!"

When Danny went to Dr. Rex's office, he weighed on the big scale again and had gained several dino pounds. His pants were no longer too big, and his dino juices had normal sugar levels according to Dr. Rex.
DR REX

Dr. Rex gave Danny a new gadget called an insulin pump. He said it would help Danny keep normal sugar levels and would reduce the number of finger pricklies that Danny would need.

Danny was once again sleeping well, playing with friends, and enjoying a wonderful life in Dinoland.

He was able to do everything his friends could do all while controlling his type 1 diabetes.

Danny Dino went on to live a dinomite life in Dinoland. He was so thankful for Dr. Rex, his friends, and his family who helped him learn how to live a happy and healthy lifestyle with diabetes.

A Guide for Parents

Whether a child is newly diagnosed or has had diabetes for quite some time, they likely still have questions about their condition and management. As you read Danny the Diabetic Dinosaur, help your child to make comparisons to their diabetes management. How did they feel when they got diagnosed? Do they see similarities in their own life to Danny's? Help them to grasp the concepts of insulin and glucose. Do they know that glucose comes from food and insulin comes from their medication? Do they understand that they need glucose for energy? Discuss the appropriate sugar levels for them based on their doctor's recommendations. Your child may also want you to journal their food like Danny does in the story. Make a list with your child of the best foods they could eat throughout the day, then take them grocery shopping the next time you go. Help them to pick out foods that would be good choices for them and their diabetes. The most important part of reading together is having fun and learning. Ask them about any questions they have about Danny or themselves, and do your best to answer them. Maybe you don't know all the answers to their questions. That is okay. Children don't expect lengthy medical explanations, they just want to be included in the process and feel heard. Next time you check their blood sugars, let your child wipe their finger off with the alcohol wipe, or let them hold the glucose monitor. Make connections to the story when you can throughout the next few days and weeks. Write down your child's questions and your own for the next time you see their provider or talk to a diabetes educator. Most importantly, relax, and know that you are going to develop a smooth routine that works for you and your child.

Disclaimer: This book is meant to be used as a learning resource and not as medical advice. Diabetes management is specific to the individual and requires a medical professional to evaluate, diagnose, and manage.